·ANIMALS ILLUSTRATED·

Walrus

·ANIMALS ILLUSTRATED·
Walrus

by Herve Paniaq • illustrated by Ben Shannon

INHABIT
MEDIA

Published by Inhabit Media Inc.
www.inhabitmedia.com

Inhabit Media Inc. (Iqaluit), P.O. Box 11125, Iqaluit, Nunavut, X0A 1H0
(Toronto), 191 Eglinton Avenue East, Suite 301, Toronto, Ontario, M4P 1K1

Design and layout copyright © 2017 Inhabit Media Inc.
Text copyright © 2017 by Herve Paniaq
Illustrations by Ben Shannon copyright © 2017 Inhabit Media Inc.

Editors: Neil Christopher, Kelly Ward, Kathleen Keenan
Art Director: Danny Christopher
Designer: Astrid Arijanto

We acknowledge the support of the Canada Council for the Arts for our publishing program.

This project was made possible in part by the Government of Canada.

ISBN: 978-1-77227-142-3

Printed in Canada

Library and Archives Canada Cataloguing in Publication

Paniaq, Herve, 1933-, author
Walrus / by Herve Paniaq ; illustrated by Ben Shannon.

(Animals illustrated)
ISBN 978-1-77227-142-3 (hardcover)

1. Walrus--Juvenile literature. I. Shannon, Ben, illustrator
II. Title. III. Series: Animals illustrated

QL737.P62P36 2017   j599.79'9   C2017-902788-3

Canada | Canada Council for the Arts   Conseil des Arts du Canada

Table of Contents

The Walrus

The walrus is a very large mammal that lives in the Arctic Ocean. Walruses are best known for the long tusks that grow from their mouths. Both male and female walruses have tusks, which can reach more than 3 feet (about 1 metre) in length. Male walruses are called "bulls" and female walruses are called "cows."

Walruses can weigh between 1,200 and 3,500 pounds (544 and 1,588 kilograms). They are mostly brown in colour, with thick, leathery skin. Male walruses are usually lighter in colour and bigger than females.

Let's learn more about walruses!

Range

Walruses live in the Arctic Ocean. They can be found in many places around the world that are close to the Arctic Circle. In Canada, walruses are found in Nunavut. In the spring and summer, many walruses can be found in the waters around the community of Igloolik.

Walruses spend a lot of time resting on ice floes on top of the ocean. They prefer to be on thinner ice that they can break with their tusks.

Skeleton

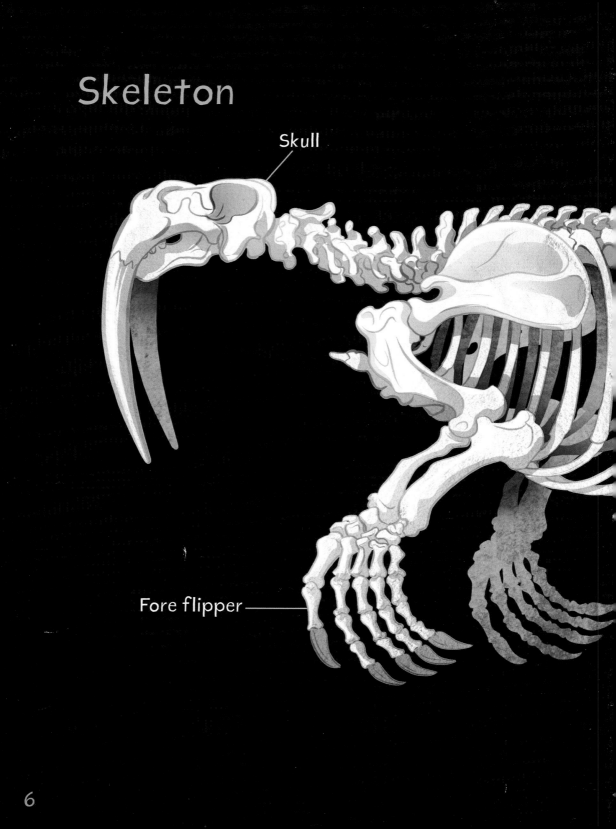

Skull

Fore flipper

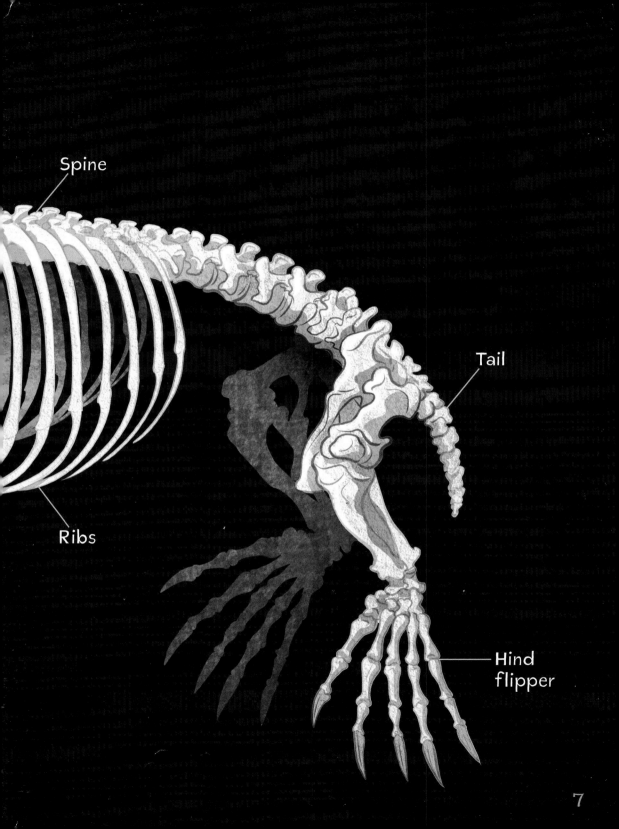

Spine

Tail

Ribs

Hind
flipper

7

Tusks

A walrus's ivory tusks, which are actually large teeth, have many uses. Walruses can use their tusks as anchors on the ice to keep themselves in one spot. When they are in the water, they can use their tusks to break open the ice from below so that they can breathe.

Tusks are also useful protection against animals that might like to hunt walruses, such as polar bears. It is said that orcas are afraid to hunt adult walruses because of their large tusks!

Whiskers and Flippers

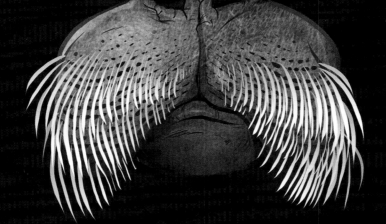

Walruses also have long, stiff whiskers around their mouths and tusks. These whiskers help them find food on the ocean floor.

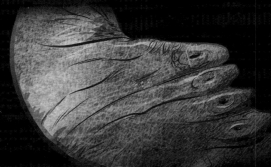

Walrus skin might look bald and leathery, but that skin is actually covered in tiny hairs! Flippers are the only parts of a walrus's body that are not covered in these tiny hairs. The smooth, hairless flippers help walruses move quickly through the water.

Diet

Walruses eat mainly small creatures—like clams and mussels—that are found on the ocean floor. Because the water is usually murky and dark, walruses use their whiskers to help them find food. They root through the ocean floor using their very sensitive whiskers to find their meals.

Walruses have been known to feed on the ocean floor for up to 79 hours straight, stopping only to breathe at the surface. During feeding time, one walrus can eat thousands of clams! Sometimes, walruses have also been known to catch fish and seals to eat. Walruses that live in very deep water are said to enjoy eating seals.

Arctic cod

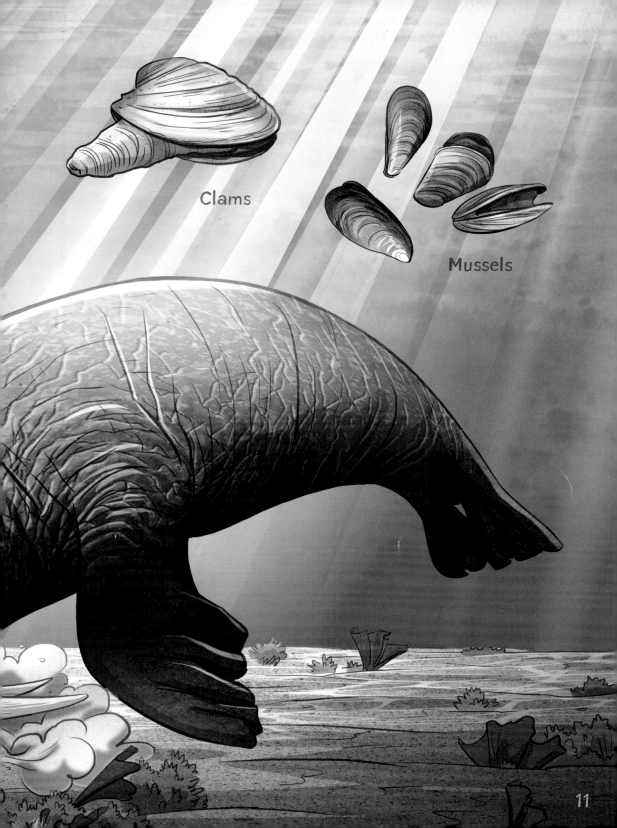

Clams

Mussels

Babies

Baby walruses are called "calves," and they are usually born in the springtime. Newborn calves are very large at birth. They can weigh up to 165 pounds (about 75 kilograms)!

Calves can swim right after they are born, but they rely on their mothers' milk for more than a year.

Predators

Because walruses are very big and have threatening tusks, they do not have many natural predators. "Predators" are the animals that try to catch and eat them.

Orcas and polar bears are the only natural predators of walruses. Both orcas and polar bears like to hunt calves or injured and weak walruses. Healthy adult walruses are much harder to catch because of their thick skin and sharp tusks.

Sometimes when a polar bear attacks a walrus, the battle
can last for many hours, and can end with the polar bear
being injured instead of the walrus.

Social Animals

Walruses are very social animals. They are usually found in large groups called "herds." Walrus herds are often separated by gender, which means that bulls and cows form separate herds.

Walrus bulls can be very aggressive to each other when they are looking for cows to mate with. They can also become aggressive when they are battling for the best position within the herd. Walruses battle with their tusks, and these fights can become bloody. Usually the biggest walrus with the longest tusks has

Fun Facts

Walruses move slowly on land, but they swim quickly. A walrus can swim just over 4 miles (about 6 kilometres) per hour. Some have even been known to swim over 21 miles (about 34 kilometres) per hour.

While they are swimming, walruses can stay awake for a long time, sometimes as long as 3 days. But on land, walruses sleep a lot. Some walruses have been seen sleeping for up to 19 hours at a time!

Blubber layer

To stay warm when they are swimming in the very cold waters of the Arctic, walruses can slow down their heartbeat. Walruses also have thick layers of fat called "blubber" that help them stay warm.

Sometimes, walruses use big pieces of ice to travel long distances. They climb onto the ice and sleep as the ice drifts across the ocean. When they wake up, they look for food in their new location.

Dangerous Creatures

Aggressive bulls and bulls that are on their own, not in a herd, can be quite dangerous to people. Some walruses have been known to attack boats. Bulls that are floating high in the water, showing a lot of their bodies above the surface, are said to be ones to look out for.

Traditional Uses

Inuit hunt walruses for food. One way of preparing walrus meat is to let it age underground. In Inuktitut, meat that is aged underground is called "*igunaq.*" Igunaq is wrapped in walrus hide and buried in the ground, to be dug up and eaten several months later. Many people love the taste of this aged meat, but it does have a very strong smell.

Traditional Inuit harpoon heads were made from the strong ivory of walrus tusks. Inuit were able to shape and sharpen the ivory to make very strong hunting tools.

Herve Paniaq is an elder from Igloolik, Nunavut.

Ben Shannon is a Canada-born, award-winning illustrator, animator, and father of two. An alumni of Sheridan College's illustration program, Ben has worked for numerous high-profile clients, including *National Geographic*, *Rolling Stone*, *the Globe and Mail*, *the Wall Street Journal*, Nike, Universal Music, Marvel, and DC Comics. Winner of the ADCC Interactive Design Illustration award in 2008, and the Applied Arts award of excellence in the field of illustration in 1998, his work was also nominated for a Canadian Screen Award in 2014. Ben is currently employed by the Canadian Broadcasting Corporation by day and is a contributing artist to the First Nations comic anthology *Moonshot* by night.

www.inhabitmedia.com

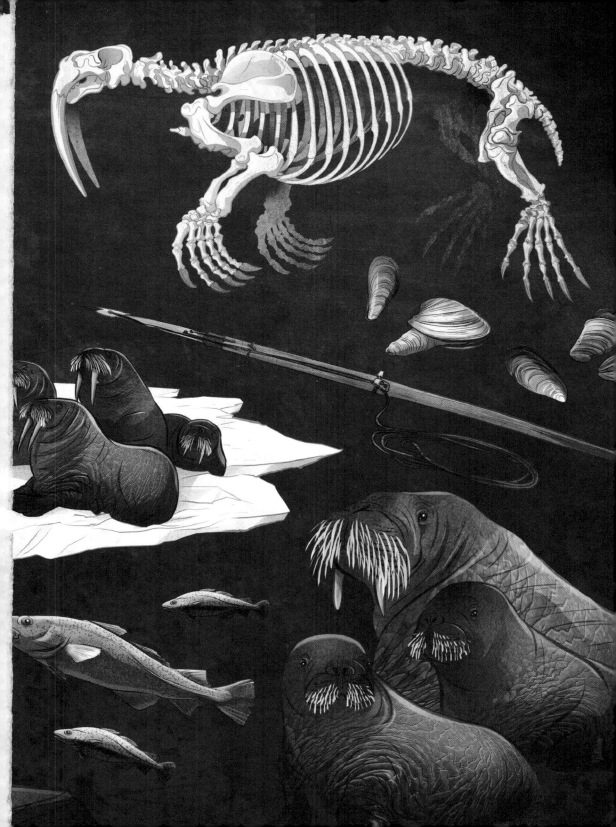

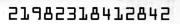